SETTING GOALS AND SUPPORTING GOAL SETTING

KEVIN EIKENBERRY

Participant Workbook

Pfeiffer

A Wiley Imprint
www.pfeiffer.com

Participant Workbook ISBN 978-0-470-50191-7
Facilitator's Guide Set ISBN 978-0-470-50557-1

Acquiring Editor: Holly J. Allen   Developmental Editor: Susan Rachmeler
Assistant Editor: Lindsay Morton   Production Editor: Michael Kay
Marketing Manager: Tolu Babalola   Manufacturing Supervisor: Becky Morgan
Director of Development: Kathleen Dolan Davies

Printed in the United States of America
Printing   10 9 8 7 6 5 4 3 2 1

Contents

THE COMPETENCIES OF
REMARKABLE LEADERS

The Remarkable Leadership workshop series is based on the book *Remarkable Leadership: Unleashing Your Leadership Potential One Skill at a Time* and consists of twelve workshops, based on thirteen leadership competencies from the book. (There is no workshop for the first competency, learn continually, as that competency is embedded in all the workshops.) Although you may not be attending the full series of workshops, all thirteen competencies are listed next.

Remarkable Leaders . . .

1. Learn Continually

2. Champion Change

3. Communicate Powerfully

4. Build Relationships

5. Develop Others

6. Focus on Customers

7. Influence with Impact

8. Think and Act Innovatively

9. Value Collaboration and Teamwork

10. Solve Problems and Make Decisions

11. Take Responsibility/Accountability

12. Manage Projects and Processes Successfully

13. **Set Goals and Support Goal Setting**

WORKSHOP OBJECTIVES

After completing this workshop, you will

- Understand the importance of goal setting.

- Know the keys to developing a goal-setting mindset.

- Understand how to create collaborative goals as a goal-setting leader.

- Know the power of and how to create alignment.

Ponder, and then write your answers:

1. What do I hope to gain from this session?

2. How often/successfully do I set goals?

3. What gets in my way?

SELF-ASSESSMENT

Here is a quick assessment to help you think about your goal setting skills.

Use the following 1–7 scale on each question:

1 – Almost never   5 – Usually

2 – Rarely/Seldom   6 – Frequently

3 – Occasionally   7 – Almost always

4 – Sometimes

I set goals.   ___

I help my team(s) set goals.   ___

I support the goals of my team(s).   ___

I help people see the big picture.   ___

I make sure all goals have plans,
measures, and milestones.   ___

THE IMPORTANCE OF GOAL SETTING

"Man is by nature a goal-striving being. And because man is 'built that way' he is not happy unless he is functioning as he was made to function—as a goal striver. Thus true success and true happiness not only go together, but each enhances the other."

~Maxwell Maltz, in *Psycho Cybernetics*

- Creates personal alignment

- Creates engagement

- Creates meaning

- Creates better results

KEYS TO A SUCCESSFUL
GOAL-SETTING MINDSET

- Size

- Belief

- Investment

- Commitment

- Action

- Purpose

Creating a Vision

The typical organizational approach is for leaders to decide on the goals and then communicate them to the people responsible for achieving them.

To be the most motivating, team goals must be co-created by the team.

As the leader, you provide the context. To provide the context, invest some time thinking about

- Your wishes and hopes for your team/organization?

- The future of your industry?

- Technological changes that might impact you?

- New opportunities?

Creating Collaborative Goals

Why?

- To gain agreement
- To set collective consciousness
- To create engagement
- To manifest synergy

Provide Ongoing Support

- Be a role model by being a goal setter yourself.
- Listen to their concerns and help them remove obstacles.
- Provide resources when possible.
- Value and use their expertise.
- Keep their focus on the big picture.
- Celebrate all successes (large and small).

■ Size makes a difference

■ Your alignment story

■ Alignment creates

  • Energy

  • Synergy

  • Magic!

CREATING ALIGNMENT

- Understand the alignment yourself.

- Ask people.

- Create conversation.

- Identify examples.

- Make a list.

- Check your list for alignment.

- Be willing to eliminate.

CREATING A PROCESS

This competency is about more than setting goals. It's really about goal achievement. Remarkable Leaders make goal setting and goal achievement an integral part of their work processes.

To create and maintain a process for goal setting and achievement, you need to

- Keep the picture clear.

- Communicate continually.

- Invest time personally.

- Be enthusiastic.

- Track progress.

The Goal-Setting Leader

1. Spend some time thinking about the vision for your team. Brainstorm and capture your thoughts regarding what is possible and desirable for your team. Think about it from your perspective, your customer's perspective, the organization's perspective, and your team's perspective. Make some notes in your journal, and continue with step 2 in a couple of days.

2. Review your work. Look back at the personal visioning exercise you did for your team; make any adjustments and clarifications that you see. Make sure you haven't been overly prescriptive. Remember that your team's success will be much more difficult if you set the goals before involving the team.

3. Meet with the team and begin the *collaborative* goal-setting process. After you've completed these visioning steps, you are ready to have a conversation with the team. (You might also consider asking each team member to do his or her own personal visioning process for the team.)

Note: It doesn't matter when this exercise takes place. Don't worry about your formal organizational goal-setting calendar. Recognize where you are now, and focus on how you can move forward from today. Of course, this exercise will be valuable leading into your calendar or fiscal year, but you can start anytime. No matter the time of year, it will be more valuable to *do it now*, than to wait for the "right" time. *No excuses!*

The Power of Alignment

Creating greater alignment within your team is an important task, to be sure. Following the steps in this section will take some time. Because Now Steps are designed to be things you can get started on "now," your team's success starts with you (no matter your position or job title).

1. Look at the alignment between your work and the team's and organization's goals and objectives. Sit down with your journal and list how your tasks relate to these goals. If you find items that aren't in alignment, investigate how you might be able to eliminate these tasks.

2. Use your personal exercise as the impetus to start this process with the whole team. Use your experiences as a model for others to do the same.

3. Make time in your team calendar to look at alignment from the group perspective.

YOUR NEXT STEPS

1. Think back to your goals for being here (page 2). Reflect on what you have learned that you can apply to your situation.

2. Teach a colleague (or your team) this content as a way to solidify your own knowledge and understanding.

3. Be responsible for applying these concepts and ideas in your work and the rest of your life.

4. Ask yourself: "Which Now Steps will I apply *right now?*"

5. Take that action!

6. Commit to your daily application to lock in your learning and achieve greater results!

"We move toward our potential when we turn learning into action."

~Kevin Eikenberry

ADDITIONAL RESOURCES

More goal setting tips are available at **www.RLBonus.com**.

- For some ideas for how to get started with personal goal setting, use the keywords "getting started."

- To get a template of these steps for goal setting and getting, use the keywords "goal template."

- For some creative ways to make the goal compelling and visible, use the keywords "compelling vision."